SURVIVAL
GUIDE

Authenticity

Persuasion

Influence

Differentiation

101 Eloqui Tips
For Successful Speaking

Second Edition

Deborah Shames · David Booth

ISBN-13: 978-0-9787594-0-7
ISBN-10: 0-9787594-0-0

Cover and interior design by NewmanGrace Inc.
Authors' photograph copyright © Ken Newman

WHETHER YOU STAND IN FRONT of a large room and prepare to deliver an important presentation; give a toast at a friend's wedding; or are asked at a networking meeting what sets you apart—you will most likely experience the number one fear in America: public speaking.

For most of us, it doesn't matter if it's an audience of our peers or a room full of strangers. Expectations are high. Suddenly, your mouth is dry, your suit no longer fits, your voice sounds odd, and you forget all the brilliant things you wanted to say. At that moment, demonstrating confidence, ease of delivery and having inspirational words is as easy as climbing Mt. Everest. It is enormously difficult to be a true representation of yourself when all eyes are upon you.

This book is an emergency kit to avert disaster. Every speaker needs safety nets, especially in those first critical moments, when anxiety can skyrocket. Like a seasoned performer or trained actor, a speaker can develop specific methods to manage anxiety. When it's built into muscle memory, even the shyest of actors rely on reflex, and deliver their lines with confidence and ease. Applied techniques provide these safety nets and as an unexpected benefit, allow the presenter to appear authentic. Consider George Burns' axiom: "Acting is all about honesty. If you can fake that, you've got it made."

Public speaking is not natural for most of us. Many believe you are born with the gift or not. We don't agree. Anyone can learn to be a compelling speaker—

iii

with training, a melding of art and science, and the commitment to authenticity.

What doesn't work is copying outdated business models that dictate how to construct content, move in a space and gesture. Models or templates don't take into account that we like anomalies, we are attracted to individual styles and we are captivated by someone who seems to be enjoying the experience.

There is also the belief that the best speakers are polished. Not true. We like to see the rough edges. When you think on your feet how best to connect with us—we're engaged. When you're comfortable speaking and use self effacing humor, rather than jokes—you make us comfortable listening to you. And when you demonstrate passion for your subject—we assume you display the same passion for your chosen profession.

Great speaking is a layering process. We know from cognitive science that in stressful situations, our tendency is to fall back on the default mode. (The behavior you have always exhibited, whether it's effective or not.) The way to combat that tendency is to start simply, incorporating one technique at a time, so that your skill level grows naturally and has integrity.

Before your next presentation, open the tip book, choose one and use it. See how it feels. Note how your audience responds. And then make an adjustment. Learning any new skill takes time, discipline and patience.

When we directed film, television, and theatre, we never considered the applica-

iv

tion of performer techniques for business professionals. Yet it makes perfect sense. Like any good actor or performer, when you deliver a presentation, you first consider your objective or what you want to achieve; decide on a role to best achieve your objective (motivator, seasoned veteran, expert); strive to engage your audience; and deal with anxiety so that it challenges—rather than paralyzes you.

We've translated performance techniques for speakers and reduced them to manageable bites. As your presentation approaches, the typical behavior is to rehearse obsessively, which only serves to make you stale. Even worse is trying to reconstruct your entire presentation immediately before going on stage, which heightens anxiety because of the fear that you will undoubtedly forget something important. Instead of going over the entire presentation, this book will sharpen your focus by directing you to take simple actions.

Whether you want to differentiate yourself in business, engage an audience, use movement as physical grammar, or properly warm up your voice, these speaker tips will serve as your guide. They allow you to develop your own shorthand and most importantly, find your authentic voice.

WE WISH TO THANK JACK GRAPES, a reformed actor and Method writing teacher, who taught us to "write like you talk."

To our muse, Dr. Lilli Friedland, who identified the source of our unique perspective: translating our experience as director and performer into the Eloqui method.

To Jeff Prather, who over an excellent bottle of Pinot Noir uncovered the essence of eloquence, resulting in the name of our company.

Our thanks to Bob Dickman, who connected the application of narrative to business communication.

To our friends in improv: Ken Newman, Kurt Bodden and William Hall, who shared their expertise and techniques to develop neural fast twitch muscles.

To Dr. Mark Goulston, who rode his motorcycle onto our doorstep to sharpen our wits and resolve.

To Dr. Peter Desberg, our guide through the labyrinth of the mind, who made us prove our theories, and back them up with anecdotal evidence.

 To our long time mentors, Dr. Lonnie Barbach, who asked the hard questions, and Sheri Adams, dear friend and extraordinary business advisor.

Many thanks to Jim Freedman, who said, almost in passing, "You should send out some kind of regular newsletter or tips to your clients." We are grateful.

To Jerri and Brian Hemsworth, who turned straw into gold with this book design and fount of creative ideas.

Finally, we are inspired by the eloquence of Ralph Waldo Emerson, who said, "It is proof of high culture to say the greatest matters in the simplest way."

Deborah Shames
David Booth

Contents

Manage Stagefright

Embrace the Fear
State Dependent Learning
High Anxiety
Judgment
On Belay
Expect Surprises
Focal Point
The Critic Speaks
Default Mode

TIP 1 EMBRACE THE FEAR

Contrary to popular belief, stage fright is beneficial. The heightened sense of awareness, total focus, and being in the moment all help a speaker be their best. Trying to achieve a Buddha-like calm can result in a boring presentation. But anxiety must be managed and channeled into useful energy. Put your full attention on engaging your audience, rather than your perceived shortcomings. Also, consider the task at hand, focus on what you want to achieve and visualize yourself as successful.

Nothing contributes so much to tranquilizing the mind as steady purpose—a point on which the soul may fix its intellectual eye.

Mary Wollstonecraft Shelley, Author of *Frankenstein*

Anxiety is a thin stream of fear trickling through the mind. If encouraged, it cuts a channel into which all other thoughts are drained.

Robert Albert Bloch, Author of *Psycho*

2

The best way to mitigate stage fright is to practice in an environment as close as possible to where you will actually be presenting. Become familiar with the particulars including the size of the room, seating arrangement and physical relationship to the audience. Rehearse standing, not seated, if you will be standing to present. Imagine the audience and make eye contact from one section to another. Adapt your voice and physical presence to the scale of the room. If speaking at a podium, rehearse with a "set piece" that approximates the height and width of the podium. Whenever possible, walk the actual space, rehearse with PowerPoint and check your microphone.

Our doubts are traitors and cause us to miss the good we oft might win by fearing to attempt.

William Shakespeare, Playwright

3

Stage fright for most speakers is a very real condition. To conquer this phobia, eliminate all distractions before presenting. Think of the benefit or value you bring to the audience. Gently warm up your voice. Practice yoga alternate breathing, or slowly breathe in through the nose and out the mouth. Begin with a personal opening you have down cold. Speak in a conversational, genuine style—as opposed to becoming more formal, structured or "businesslike." And remember one thing. What do I want to accomplish?

Present fears are less than horrible imaginings.

William Shakespeare, Playwright

Speakers often assume incorrectly that the audience is judging them harshly and expecting them to fail. This not only increases anxiety, but results in playing it safe with content and delivery. An audience simply wants to be engaged. We appreciate speakers who appear genuine, know their subject matter and creatively convey their message. Maintain the courage of your convictions and if you feel anxious, focus on the people in the audience who are giving you positive feedback.

A successful person is one who can lay a firm foundation with the bricks that others throw at him.

David Brinkley, TV Newscaster

Sherpas cross perilous chasms by imagining a taut string from their navel to the other side. When mountain climbing, team members rope themselves together. When you speak, establish that invisible connection and keep it taut throughout the presentation.

Connecting will keep you focused and is palpable to the audience. Make eye contact, be receptive and stay locked in, physically and mentally. Your strength and courage of conviction will be evident and persuasive.

> *… Apply discipline to your thoughts when they become anxious over the outcome of a goal. Impatience breeds anxiety, fear, discouragement and failure. Patience creates confidence, decisiveness, and a rational outlook, which eventually leads to success.*
>
> Brian Adams, Filmmaker

EXPECT SURPRISES

No matter how well you prepare your presentation, chances are there will be surprises. Your PowerPoint or remote will fail. The microphone will screech or pop. The room or audience size will be different than expected. Your time to speak will suddenly change. And the decision maker will enter, or leave the room. Instead of letting these changes affect your performance, use them to your advantage. Step out in front—literally and figuratively. Go "low tech." Use a flip chart or white board, instead of the failed PowerPoint. Demonstrate flexibility and self effacing humor. You will be remembered for your confidence and admired for your ability to handle a difficult situation.

When you come to a fork in the road, take it.

Yogi Berra, Baseball Player and Manager

I wanted a perfect ending. Now I've learned, the hard way, that some poems don't rhyme, and some stories don't have a clear beginning, middle, and end. Life is about not knowing, having to change, taking the moment and making the best of it, without knowing what's going to happen next.

Gilda Radner, Comedienne

Speakers experience heightened anxiety when they focus inward on their perceived inadequacies, instead of outward on the audience. When actors congratulate or critique themselves during a performance, they inevitably "dry up" and forget their lines. This may be a shock, but it's not about you. It's about your message. To be a successful speaker, direct your attention to the audience and what will most engage them. They will feel the effect of your concentrated focus and your anxiety will be reduced.

We have another ear that never ceases. It's as sensitive as can be. You're working with your fellow actors but that other ear, that other antenna hears the audience—always.

Carol Channing, Actress

THE CRITIC SPEAKS

Most of us are acutely concerned about how we will be perceived and our talk received. If you avoid speaking opportunities; spend an inordinate amount of time preparing, rehearsing and panicking over an upcoming presentation; or worry about being judged harshly, you are not alone. Techniques to reduce these anxieties include: present in a conversational tone as close to your natural style as possible; redirect the critic in your head to finding multiple ways to engage your audience; craft and rehearse your opening; and envision the audience applauding or engaging your services.

> *Women have been trained to speak softly and carry a lipstick. Those days are over.*
>
> Bella Abzug, New York Congresswoman

Changing speech habits is a wrestling match. When an environment is stressful, or the stakes are high, we tend to fall back on the familiar. Specifically, speakers tend to say too much, use PowerPoint as a crutch, or read from a completely prepared text. To energize your presentation, focus on what you're passionate about. Create visual snapshots. Incorporate intelligent metaphors or descriptive anecdotes. And vary your pace. By pushing yourself into the unfamiliar, you create a sense of immediacy, while flexing new muscles. Incorporate one new tool at a time, until being unpredictable becomes your new default.

A great deal of chaos occurs in the world because people don't appreciate themselves.

Chogyam Trungpa, Tibetan Buddhist philosopher

The Art Of Narrative

Spin A Yarn
Framing
Openings
Momentum
Storytelling
Then and Now
Musicality
Finale

In business, the challenge is making technical information stick. When data is embedded in a story, it will more readily be placed into long term memory. This narrative need not be linear, though it must contain a beginning, middle and end. Consider Robert Dickman's definition of a story as "fact wrapped in emotion." Describe challenges or obstacles followed by creative solutions. Include what makes the characters or players worth caring about. Who is the hero and the antagonist? Are there vivid details? And is there a satisfying resolution? Like any good story, client anecdotes need contour and shape to illuminate the message.

> *Developing excellent communication skills is absolutely essential to effective leadership. The leader must be able to share knowledge and ideas to transmit a sense of urgency and enthusiasm to others. If a leader can't get a message across clearly and motivate others to act on it, then having a message doesn't even matter.*
>
> Gilbert Amelio, CEO

TIP 11   FRAMING

When preparing your presentation, consider the visual snapshot, metaphor or simile that leads your remarks. Be sure the frame serves your purpose, for it will become your reference point. For example, a lawyer compared a trademark to a house—which requires a contract and can be leased, bought or sold. This metaphor also suggests other qualities of a house, e.g. pride of ownership, protection for your family and implied wealth. Choose a frame carefully, because like a painting, this device becomes the border for the content contained within.

... what cognitive linguists call a "frame"... is a mental structure that we use in thinking. All words are defined relative to frames....The hero is inherently good, the villain is evil and the victim after the rescue owes gratitude to the hero.

George Lakoff, Author of *Metaphors We Live By*

13

TIP 12   **OPENINGS**

To engage your audience, eliminate wind-ups or fillers. These include "Thank you for having me", "Over the next few minutes I will cover", or "The agenda of my presentation will be…." Instead, reveal your unique take on the subject, or why you're passionate about it. Dive into your topic without prelude or explanation. It should have the feeling of falling off a cliff, so the audience is immediately drawn in. If you have to thank your host or introduce yourself, place these remarks after your unique opening and once you have captured their attention. Remember, attention precedes comprehension.

Do not promote what you can't explain, simplify, and prove early.

Louis Pasteur, Scientist

Pacing, rhythm and timing are building blocks to great storytelling. Compelling narrative builds excitement until it reaches a climax and resolves details in a final wrap up. Strive to relate anecdotes with the same tension. Don't allow the listener to lose interest by revealing too soon how the tale ends—or how you solved the problem. Create momentum by jumping into the meat of the story. Sustain the tension and build toward a crescendo. Being conscious of momentum will build your storytelling muscle, ensure your story is memorable, and extend your reach beyond the initial telling.

Storytelling reveals meaning without committing the error of defining it.

Hannah Arendt, Political Scientist and Philosopher

TIP 14 STORYTELLING

Well told narratives are typically the way we learn about our origin, history, environment, and culture—passed down from one generation to the next. Key story elements include a compelling open and close; complex characters; obstacles or challenges; transformation of the hero through lessons learned; recurrent theme; vibrant pacing; and a colorful delivery. The more technical the information, the more storytelling techniques can enliven and make it memorable.

The preacher's voice was beautiful. He told us about the sufferings of the natives, and he pleaded for help with such moving simplicity that I mentally doubled the fifty cents I had intended to put in the plate. He described the pitiful misery of those savages so vividly that the dollar I had in mind gradually rose to five. Then that preacher continued, and I felt that all the cash I had carried on me would be insufficient, and I decided to write a large check. Then he went on and I abandoned the idea of the check. And he went on, and I got back to five dollars. And he went on, and I back to four, two, one. And still he went on. And when the plate came around, I took ten cents out of it.

Mark Twain, Writer

TIP 15 THEN AND NOW

When relating a case study or anecdote, even though the event has already occurred, set up the context and then use dialogue in the present tense, e.g. "I have a client who was devastated in the tech wreck. When his portfolio lost 90% of its value, he stared at his computer screen and said: Why did I think I could manage my own investments?! I've lost my kids' college tuition." Instead of reporting on an event and observing from a distance, this dialogue form creates immediacy. Bringing the past into the present gives your narrative dynamic energy and allows the listener to experience the story for themselves.

We don't want tradition. We want to live in the present and the only history that is worth a tinker's damn is the history we make today.

> Henry Ford, Automaker and Captain of Industry

I have realized that the past and future are real illusions, that they exist in the present, which is what there is and all there is.

> Alan Watts, Writer and Philosopher

17

MUSICALITY

A classic piece of music contains the same elements as a memorable presentation. A recognizable melody is the equivalent of a talk's dominant theme. In classical composition, this melody is woven through each of the four movements, with different instrumentation. In a great speech, a recurring theme is revisited with variations, from change-up in tempo and emphasis, to suggesting a new perspective... Similar to the instruments in a symphony, we enjoy the counterpoint of speaking voices, playing off each other in pairs or teams... And like any professional musician, speakers need to warm up their vocal instrument to elicit vibrant tones.

> *To create by inspiration, one must be aware of one's own individuality.*
>
> Michael Chekhov, Acting Teacher

TIP 17 FINALE

How often have you heard a speaker finish with "Questions?", "Thank you" or "That's all"? To conclude your presentation dynamically, refer to or bookend the opening, bringing your talk full circle... To achieve a specific objective, deliver a call to action... For inspirational talks, quote a famous person, preferably someone who has long passed. Be familiar with the context of the quote, and how to pronounce the author's name... Choose a personal story or anecdote to reveal your values and why you are passionate about the subject... Or consider using triplicates for dramatic emphasis, e.g. "I believe", "I know" or "I envision". Triplicates signify the end of your presentation, so don't start another section after employing them. No matter how you choose to close, demonstrate commitment and certainty.

Great is the art of beginning, but greater is the art of ending.

Henry Wadsworth Longfellow, American poet

19

Structure Your Content

Intention
Less Prep Time
Never Forget
Honeymoon Period
Elephant in the Room
Visual Snapshots

Play the Movie
Italian Waiter
Humor
Grabbed from the Headlines
The Usual Suspects
Triplicate

When preparing your talk, decide on the one thing you would like to achieve. Then consider your content, and include only what supports this objective. Choosing one intention eliminates the tendency to ramble, or include too many facts and figures. Most speakers don't have an intention or have too many. Others believe their goal is to educate or inform rather than persuade and influence. If this rings true, ask yourself, "why am I speaking?" The answer will be your intention.

We succeed only as we identify in life, or in war, or in anything else, a single overriding objective, and make all other considerations bend to that one objective.

Dwight D. Eisenhower, U.S. President

When structuring a presentation, consider this template. First, determine your objective and how best to achieve it. Make this objective "active" and one sentence long, beginning with "I want" or "I will." Next, choose an opening that engages the audience and suggests a recurrent theme. For example, a lawyer's open was "When I mediate a dispute, I'm like an octopus with tentacles on the pulse of everyone in the room." His theme for the remainder of his talk was "monitoring the pulse." Next, identify the major points to include in the body of the presentation. Finally, determine how best to close.

It usually takes more than three weeks to prepare a good impromptu speech.

Mark Twain, Writer

Memory has three stages. When you pay attention to incoming information, the sensory register is engaged. Next, working (or short term) memory is attempting to process the information. If there is an associative image (metaphor, simile or anecdote), pattern recognition or the ability of the brain to rehearse it, this information will go into long term memory. When trying to remember someone's name, you can link it to a personal characteristic (e.g. curly hair for Shirley, Mark no bark), repeat it to yourself a number of times, or use it in conversation. When you spend the time to prepare a presentation, include the markers to make it memorable.

History is the version of past events that people have decided to agree upon.

Napoleon Bonaparte, French Emperor

© 2008 Second Edition, Eloqui   **Speaker Survival Guide**

TIP 21   HONEYMOON PERIOD

Audiences are keenly attuned to the beginning of any presentation. They decide quickly if a speaker is worth their time and attention. This initial 45 seconds is the Honeymoon Period—and with the right elements, can transition into a successful marriage. Move perfunctory remarks or obligatory "thank you's" to later in the presentation. Open with a visual image linked to your core thesis or idea. Ask an intriguing question. Tell a personal anecdote or reveal your unique perspective. These techniques demonstrate control and allow the audience to relax and support you.

I am only a public entertainer who has understood his time.

Pablo Picasso, Artist

TIP 22   ELEPHANT IN THE ROOM

Most of us try to avoid conflict. However, if there is an underlying problem, obstacle or contentious point, your audience will focus on this "elephant." You and your message will play second chair. Demonstrate your courage and fearlessness by getting there first. Expose the problem. Surprise them by taking the air out of the balloon. Propose solutions without defensiveness. Your audience will admire your courage and give you their attention for the rest of your talk.

Without courage, wisdom bears no fruit.

Baltasar Gracian, Spanish Jesuit philosopher

TIP 23   VISUAL SNAPSHOTS

If the audience can envision your presentation via specific, salient details, they will remember it and be engaged. Enliven your content with visual images, anecdotes, case studies, similes or metaphors. We understand ideas or objects by their relationship to something else, i.e. field and foreground. Even though the listener may not have had the same experience as you, if you create context with vivid details, they will picture your example and run it through the filter of their own experience.

The trouble with most people is that they think with their hopes or fears or wishes rather than with their minds.

Lady Nancy Astor, Socialite

I write scripts to serve as skeletons awaiting the flesh and sinew of images.

Ingmar Bergman, Swedish Film Director

26

PLAY THE MOVIE

When a speaker is compelling, the audience is riveted. Instead of running their "to do" lists or wondering how they ended up held captive, the audience plays a movie in their heads of what is being described. Similar to great photography or art, a picture is worth a thousand words. To capture this visual snapshot, the speaker needs to include specific, colorful details to engage the 30% of our cerebral cortex involved in visual processing. Done properly, listeners will recreate your text, assisted by vivid descriptors.

> *To accomplish great things, we must first dream, then visualize, then plan… believe… act!*
>
> Alfred A. Montapert, Author and Philosopher

© 2008 Second Edition, Eloqui

In formal Northern Italian restaurants, you order one course of food and eat it before ordering the next one. This process can be applied to persuasive speaking because listeners can digest only one concept at a time. It is often the first time an audience is receiving this information or your perspective. To be memorable, they need to hear it in tasty "bites." Be creative with techniques for delivering your message, so that each idea is fully explored before moving on.

If nobody spoke unless he had something to say, the human race would very soon lose the use of speech.

Somerset Maugham, British Playwright and Author

Oscar Wilde said "Dying is easy. Comedy is hard." Never begin with a joke, which asks the audience to respond with a laugh. Jokes have a high failure rate. When they don't work, they create discomfort and distance. Leave joke telling to the professionals. Self effacing humor and charm work better and draw people in. By sharing your experience or revealing something self deprecating, you display vulnerability and a willingness to laugh at yourself. This is an effective way of relaxing an audience and warming them up to you.

The essence of humor is surprise.

Aristotle, Greek Philosopher

He who laughs most, learns best.

John Cleese, British Comedic Actor

TIP 27   GRABBED FROM THE HEADLINES

Audiences respond to a speaker who appears spontaneous. One method to create this sense of immediacy is to begin with a current news item that you can link to your topic, but does not necessarily have an obvious application. Be sure the story has an emotional charge for you. Describe only the highlights—then segue into your topic. Opening with a news story provides a unique slant and shows you have tailored your talk specifically to the audience. And as a bonus, if the link to your topic is insightful, you gain respect and a hunger to hear more.

There is in the act of preparing that moment when you start caring.

Winston Churchill, British Prime Minister

THE USUAL SUSPECTS

In this movie, Kevin Spacey's character is detained by the police. Waiting to be interrogated, he sits in an office, selecting items off a bulletin board to comprise his fictional character's back story. Speakers can use the same technique to capture our attention. In a live presentation, pick up on signals you see and hear from the client. Scan the paraphernalia on a client's office wall, or the company's website for a recent announcement or press release, which you then fold into the conversation. Great communicators convey a sense of immediacy, awareness and being "in the moment."

You can observe a lot by watching.

Yogi Berra, Baseball Player and Manager

TRIPLICATE

From ancient orators to Southern preachers, a dramatic way to present material is through repetition. In the U.S., the most recognized form of repetition is the triplicate. When a speaker repeats phrases, like "I know...", "We will..." or "I believe..." three times, the incantatory delivery can powerfully emphasize one's beliefs or lead a call to action. Each line should build in relevance or importance. For example: "I believe anyone can learn to speak in their own voice... I believe when people speak authentically, they are more persuasive... And I believe when this happens, the world will be transformed."

> *... You ask, what is our aim? I can answer with one word: Victory—victory at all costs, victory in spite of all terror, victory however long and hard the road may be; for without victory there is no survival.*
>
> Sir Winston Churchill, British Prime Minister

Vocalease

Your voice is a delicate instrument, and should be properly tuned. Start drinking room temperature water about an hour before speaking and eat grapes or apples for natural lubrication. Avoid dairy products and bananas, which leave your mouth sticky, as well as alcohol, coffee or black tea, which contain drying agents. For a warm-up, yawn to open your vocal folds. To vibrate your resonators for richer tones, hum "m's" or "z's" in ascending and descending scales, reaching for the highest and lowest notes in your register.

I stand in pause where I shall first begin.

William Shakespeare, Playwright

TIP 31   WHERE YOU FROM?

If you have difficulty being understood, there are techniques to sound clear and distinct. Identify a narrator of a book-on-tape whose voice you would like to emulate. Play the CD and repeat their narration aloud, following closely behind. Google and download a Shakespeare sonnet or soliloquy. Read the piece out loud, exaggerating every word as if you were chewing tough meat. To improve your diction, commit to daily exercises which you over-enunciate, like "lippity pippity," "lily let lucy," "buddagedda," or "ooo weet."

Precision of communication is important, more important than ever, in our era of hair trigger balances, when a false or misunderstood word may create as much disaster as a sudden thoughtless act.

James Thurber, Author

"Twenty dwarves took turns doing handstands on the carpet floor."

Warren Beatty, Actor in the movie Bugsy

35

Precise logic is expressed through consonants. If your p's, b's, t's and k's are sharp and clear, you will sound intelligent. Conversely, if your consonants are muddy or soft, your audience will assume the same of your thinking.... Emotional import is carried by the vowels. Consider the emphasis on vowels in Martin Luther King's famous "I have a dream" speech (see below). To convey emotional resonance, give vowels their full value. Round out and extend your a, e, i, o, and u's for added richness and impact.

> *I say to you today, my friends, so even though we face the difficulties of today and tomorrow, I still have a dream. It is a dream deeply rooted in the American dream.*
>
> Martin Luther King Jr, Civil Rights Activist

TIP 33   DISCOURSE PARTICLES

Linguists call filler words and phrases such as "um," "ah," "you know," "well," "just," "so" and "like"—discourse particles. They are used because speakers think they need to fill space while formulating a thought. Unfortunately, over time, these fillers become fixed speech patterns. And when used repeatedly, audiences begin to count them and lose the thread of your talk. Try this. When rehearsing your next presentation, repeat your discourse particle every other word until you are acutely aware of it. This awareness begins the erasure process. The goal is to replace your filler with a pause, the speaker's best friend.

Personally I'm always ready to learn, although I do not always like being taught.

Sir Winston Churchill, British Prime Minister

There are commonly used words, which are consistently mispronounced. Consider "anecdote", "recognize" and "picture". Too often we hear "anedote" (or "antidote"), "reconize" and "pitcher". This migration into a different word is confusing. It is a result of speaking too quickly, sloppy diction and leaving out a key consonant, so that the word becomes contracted or misshapen. Clear enunciation reflects clarity of thought.

But wise men pierce this rotten diction and fasten words again to visible things; so that picturesque language is at once a commanding certificate that he who employs it, is a man in alliance with truth and God.

Ralph Waldo Emerson, Author

Speakers should avoid leaning in too close or backing off too far from a microphone. The proper distance is a closed fist with a protruding thumb. Don't turn your head away from the mike, which causes you to go out of audible range. Move your body in tandem with the microphone. Speak in a conversational tone that doesn't fluctuate dramatically in volume. A common mistake is to point the microphone directly at your mouth and speak down the barrel, so that p's, b's and t's sound like exploding firecrackers. Instead, angle the microphone toward your trachea, the location which delivers the best tonal quality and picks up chest resonance.

Suit the action to the word, the word to the action; with this special observation, that you overstep not the modesty of nature.

William Shakespeare, Playwright

Speaker Survival Guide

When moving from one side of the podium to the other, reposition a fixed mount microphone during a pause, to avoid gooseneck squeaks.... Wireless or lavaliere microphones should be placed about 6" below your chin and centered on your sternum. For men, place the lavaliere on your tie and above your lapel, so it doesn't cause a swooshing sound.... For women, large rings on the hand holding the mic can cause a loud tapping noise. Necklaces rustle against a lavaliere mic. Less is more. With a hard wired mic, use one hand to comfortably hold it and the other to keep the cable out of your way. Switch hands periodically.

> *I am always starting up, straining to hear a change in the sound.*
>
> Susan Sontag, Author

TIP 37 SPRAY PAINT

Actors say "If they can't hear you, it doesn't matter how good you are—you're not in the game." For vocal projection, imagine your voice as spray paint, and you are covering the last row in the theatre. Breathe into your belly, lift and throw your voice towards the back wall with an "ah." Aim for precision, not mere volume. Practice out of doors to become accustomed to covering great distance, until your voice sounds natural and unforced. The actor Richard Burton was known to stand on the cliffs of Wales and project his sonorous voice against the roar of wind and waves.

The man who goes farthest is generally the one who is willing to do and dare. The sure-thing boat never gets far from shore.

Dale Carnegie, Business theorist and teacher

Far better it is to dare mighty things, to win glorious triumphs even though checkered by failure, than to rank with those poor spirits who neither enjoy nor suffer much because they live in the gray twilight that knows neither victory nor defeat.

Theodore Roosevelt, U.S. President

41

Delivery

TIP 38   MAKE IT COUNT

Most people spend an inordinate amount of time preparing the content for an upcoming pitch or presentation. Rarely do they put sufficient attention on the delivery. Professional theatre companies spend approximately one month rehearsing a play, constantly refining and reworking the material. If a production opens to bad reviews, it will likely fold. Allocate time to rehearse, analyze your weak points, finesse hand-offs, and build in safety nets, like revisiting your theme, prepping questions for the audience, or having a back-up plan if the PowerPoint fails. Typically you only get one at-bat on important projects.

All the world's a stage and most of us are desperately unrehearsed.

Sean O'Casey, Playwright

43

TIP 39   SELF AWARENESS

See yourself as others do. Videotape your presentation. Once past the initial shock of how much you weigh, what your hair looks like and the lines on your face, you can begin the process of refining your speaking skills. Professional athletes watch themselves ski down a mountain or serve a tennis ball as a way to improve their performance. Review your tape and concentrate on what you do well, like gesturing with your hands or making eye contact. Then focus on what you want to change like rambling, reducing your "ums" or moving without a purpose. Ultimately, watching yourself will transform self consciousness into a finely tuned awareness.

Speech is the mirror of the soul; as a man speaks, so he is.

Publilius Syrus, Roman Senator and Writer

TIP 40   STUMBLE THROUGH

As a performer, your primary objective is to be successful on opening night. A rehearsal played to the hilt just hours before the curtain rises is a recipe for disaster. The same holds true for speakers. Rather than a full run-through, which can make you peak too soon and heighten anxiety, do what actors call a "stumble through," going over the presentation quickly and delivering the highlights of the content in a cursory review. This rehearsal requires minimal emotion or investment and leaves room for improvisation. Save your best for the actual presentation.

Divest oneself of passivity.

Dr. Martin Luther King, Civil Rights Leader

To be an effective speaker, it is imperative to compose yourself and clear your head of distractions at least ten minutes prior to delivering your presentation. Actors call this "bridging" or transitioning from their own persona to the role they are about to play. Before your presentation, write down any nagging responsibilities or thoughts to handle later. Find a quiet space for relaxation exercises and deep breathing. Rehearse your opening. Drink room temperature water. If you feel anxious, remember a time when you were calm and envision yourself successful. Most importantly, remind yourself of the value you bring to the audience.

Take time to deliberate, but when the time for action has arrived, stop thinking and go in.

Napoleon Bonaparte, Emperor of France

Speaker anxiety can come from external sources. Check out the environment and walk the space where you will be presenting. If you can't be there ahead of time, call or email your contact to clarify the following: Number of attendees… Room set up… Distance from the audience and your physical proximity… Direction of natural light that could adversely affect your PowerPoint…Your place on the agenda (try to avoid being right after a meal)… And type of microphone, i.e. lavaliere, podium mounted, or hand held. Although it's impossible to eliminate all pitfalls, you can minimize their effect. Leave time to rehearse on site with your PowerPoint and always do a microphone sound check.

If I went back to college again, I'd concentrate on two areas: learning to write and to speak before an audience. Nothing in life is more important than the ability to communicate effectively.

Gerald Ford, U.S. President

47

Memorable performers eliminate distractions to be completely in the moment. Their attention is focused on the role and connecting with the audience, rather than the critic in their head. They have determined their objective, which guides every move. They actively use the space, move toward the audience to break through the invisible wall, and they may change a line reading to keep the performance fresh. Speakers can learn from stage actors. The goal of performers and speakers alike is to engage their audience.

Mastering others gives you strength. Mastering yourself makes you fearless.

Lao-Tzu, Chinese Philosopher

TIP 44 FIRST IMPRESSION

Most speakers are unaware of the image they convey with their choice of wardrobe. The traditional business attire of white shirt, dark suit and red, blue or yellow tie is appropriate if you're running for office or presenting yourself as an expert—but this high contrast uniform does not signify "let's have a conversation or business relationship." For a more approachable, engaging impression, wear colors closer to your skin tone and keep the contrast low. The idea is to direct attention to your face, not to brightly colored ties or sparkling jewelry.

> *Life is like music. It must be composed by ear, feeling and instinct, not by rule. Nevertheless, one had better know the rules, for they sometimes guide in doubtful cases, though not often.*
>
> Samuel Butler, Author

Speaker Survival Guide

TIP 45 SEE JANE READ

It is tempting to consider reading or memorizing your talk. Especially if you suffer from stage fright, reading ensures you will leave nothing out. You will also not risk sounding foolish or forget key points. However, we would rather have a speaker pause and search for the right word, than steamroll through text in a mechanical fashion. Give yourself safety nets. Rehearse with different line readings or paraphrasing. Refer to an outline and bold key words so they can be easily grabbed off the page. Make eye contact with your audience. Read their response and make adjustments. We appreciate a speaker's courage, their ability to think on their feet, and the sense of immediacy when they do their best to connect with us.

I don't know the key to success, but the key to failure is trying to please everybody.

Bill Cosby, Comedian

50

TIP 46   MAGNETISM

Engage your audience by opening up physically, e.g. facing forward, not crossing arms, legs or standing behind a podium or chair. Make direct eye contact, gesture and whenever possible, encourage people to participate. Move to make a point, and vary the distance between you and the audience. Lift a phrase by slowing down or speeding up, and underline an important point by upping your commitment and sense of resolve. Punctuate with a sharp vocal attack, and create intimacy by lowering the volume. When you are dynamic in motion and phrasing, you engage the listener.

Never confuse movement with action.

Ernest Hemingway, Author

© 2008 Second Edition, Eloqui

When you move from behind the podium, where do you go? Since actors first appeared on the Greek stage around 4 BC, the same rules apply. Proclaim your theme, or primary subject in the center of the space... Walking back and forth signifies "consider these points" or "I'm thinking..." Crossing diagonally toward the audience punctuates an important point... And moving directly toward your audience in a straight line connotes intimacy or aggression, so lower your voice. Make your movements lean, justified and economical. Suit the action to the word, using your body as well as your voice to double the impact.

The greatest ruler acts as he speaks and tailors his speech to his actions.

Confucius, Chinese Philosopher

SHOW AND TELL

Props are effective tools for engaging an audience. Since one third of the cerebral cortex is involved in visual processing, a prop gives us a visual, as well as verbal reference. Inclusion of props can be planned, or any nearby object can be picked up at an appropriate point in a presentation. A prop can represent anything. Your pen can be the direction of sales; a daily planner can reflect all the data on your company's new microchip; your eyeglasses can be your vision for the coming year. Basic rule of thumb with props is "use 'em and lose 'em." Display them briefly to make your point, and then put them down.

Speech is a picture of the mind.

John Ray, Naturalist, Philosopher and Theologian

Napoleon was known to face his troops in silence for an interminable amount of time. He waited until he had everyone's attention. He understood the power of the pause, the cornerstone of all timing. When speaking, if you want to emphasize a phrase—pause before and/or after. If you would like the impact of your statement to sink in—pause. Comics set up punch lines with a pause. Similarly, speakers can give any statement more gravity or reflection, by preceding it with a pause. Vary the length, reserving a longer silence for your critical points. Think of the pause as directing the audience's attention to a specific point and giving them time to absorb it.

> *Pauses are what make a speech sound conversational... When you pause, you sound sincere, as if you're trying to come up with the right words to express your thoughts.*
>
> James C. Humes, Speechwriter for 3 Presidents

CRAFTING HONESTY

It is ironic that employing a mechanical
device can enhance your authenticity.
Sometimes life defies logic. For example,
when speaking, if you drop your shoulders,
open your chest and slightly lift your chin,
you appear more confident and in control....
If you walk at an angle toward your
audience, it will give your statement more
impact... And if you employ an empathic
tone, you will more readily be perceived as a
trusted advisor. Consider the impression and
outcome you desire and then utilize
technique to achieve it.

*The power of accurate observation is commonly called
cynicism by those who have not got it.*

George Bernard Shaw, Irish Dramatist and Literary Critic

Speaker Survival Guide

When delivering a presentation, be aware of the non-verbal cues you telegraph. Traditional business models dictate mirroring the body language of the decision maker in the room. This can backfire, especially if you are pitching to someone more senior, who may not see you on their level. Instead, sit upright with a straight back to appear alert and engaged. Lean slightly forward to show interest. Listen intently and give full focus to show respect. Use your hands to gesture, but do not cross your arms. When standing, start in "body neutral" with hands at your sides and feet shoulder width apart. You will soon find yourself moving and gesturing to complement your content.

Insanity: doing the same thing over and over again and expecting different results.

Albert Einstein, Scientist

TIP 52 PULLING FOCUS

When presenting as part of a team, avoid drawing attention to yourself when someone else is speaking. Any physical movement or gesture pulls focus. Unintentional faux pas include: taking notes, gazing anywhere but at the speaker and worst of all, assessing the audience's reaction by making eye contact around the room. The actor Michael Caine said the most important training for an actor was how to listen. Exhibit support for the speaker by facing and listening intently to them, occasionally nodding in assent. You will, in actors' terms, be throwing and not pulling focus.

Listening, not imitation, may be the sincerest form of flattery.

Dr. Joyce Brothers, Psychologist

© 2008 Second Edition, Eloqui   **Speaker Survival Guide**

Audiences respond favorably to speakers who make strong eye contact. Look directly into peoples' eyes, unless it is unnerving or the lighting makes this impossible. In that case, stare at their foreheads—which appears as if you're looking directly at them. Don't rest your gaze for more than a few seconds, or the recipient will be uncomfortable. Change the sequence and vary the length of your eye contact. When thinking of what to say, look out at the audience, instead of down or away. When all else fails, find the individuals who show genuine interest and make regular eye contact with them.

If you don't say anything, you won't be called upon to repeat it.

Calvin Coolidge, U.S. President

The good news is that we have been using language for most of our lives. The bad news is that over time, we have become habituated to a single style of speaking. To break out of familiar speech patterns and enliven your delivery, rehearse your talk as a motivational speaker, over-the-top actor, or field general. Choose the voice and body language of a fictional character—as different from you as possible. Allow yourself the freedom to play without constraints. What's different? Do you feel looser? How does this character affect your voice and gestures? What can you take from this exercise when you deliver your talk in your own voice?

Consistency is the last refuge of the unimaginative.
Oscar Wilde, Playwright

Prefrontal cortical activity is a strong predictor of idea generation and overall liveliness of thought. When you're thinking on your feet, when you're full of ideas, your frontal lobes are firing on all cylinders.
Steven Johnson, Author of *Mind Wide Open*

59

The disclaimer at the end of a car commercial races through legal copy to avoid liability. When a speaker races through their content, it connotes a lack of importance and commitment. Speed telegraphs the message "I will be finished as quickly as possible." A slower, measured pace is considerate, thoughtful and gives your audience the chance to digest the material. Vary the rate, rhythm and pacing of your presentation, but always have the speed under control.

If you think you're boring your audience, go slower, not faster.

Gustav Mahler, Composer

PUNCH IT!

Whereas the opening of your presentation sets the tone—your final remarks are what will be remembered. When finishing, don't lower your voice, mumble or speed up and waste the opportunity to make a lasting impression. Take charge and employ a bit of dramatic emphasis. Slow down and make every word count. Move your gaze around the room. Be definitive and never back off from your commitment. Whenever possible, inject your own feelings or perspective to deliver the strongest emotional component.

What convinces is conviction. Believe in the argument you're advancing. If you don't you're as good as dead. The other person will sense that something isn't there, and no chain of reasoning, no matter how logical or elegant or brilliant, will win your case for you.

Lyndon B. Johnson, U.S. President

TIP 57   KEEP IT FRESH

When you repeat slogans, mottos, tag lines or your company's features and benefits, trick your brain into hearing and delivering the material as though it were new. First, speak the lines the way you always do. Then place the pauses and emphases in all the wrong places... Jumble or mix up the order of the phrases... Deliver the material in a bad French accent, in an operatic style, or as a rapper... Dance it... Speak to an audience of five year olds—then seniors who are hard of hearing... Immediately thereafter, speak in a normal voice and listen for the difference.

Do not be too timid and squeamish about your actions. All life is an experiment. The more experiments you make the better. What if they are a little coarse, and you may get your coat soiled or torn? What if you do fail, and get fairly rolled in the dirt once or twice. Up again, you shall never be so afraid of a tumble.

Ralph Waldo Emerson, Author

Business Speak

When structuring and delivering a presentation, be acutely aware of what you want to accomplish. Is your goal to influence a strategic decision, land a job, or gain the attention of a potential client? If you find yourself copying other speakers, delivering too much data, or going off point, it's likely you're on autopilot and have veered from your course. Grab the helm. Pose a robust theory, engage the audience in a dialogue, reorder your content, turn off the PowerPoint and speak from your experience. Keep focused on the outcome, instead of following a prescribed template. Being nimble allows changes midstream and increases your odds of success.

Our task is not to fix the blame for the past, but to fix the course for the future.

John F. Kennedy, U.S. President

TIP 59   MESSAGING

Before relating a client anecdote, telling someone what you do, or going on camera for a media interview—first determine the message (or underlying concept) you would like to deliver. Do you want to convey your creativity in solving problems? Describe the business challenges that are your sweet spot? Or express the urgency to donate to your favorite charity? Once you know the take-a-way, you can artfully weave that message into your narrative for maximum effect. Rule of thumb: one message per presentation.

Regardless of the changes in technology, the market for well-crafted messages will always have an audience.

Steve Burnett, Author on technology topics

Speaker Survival Guide

Many business professionals call themselves trusted advisors. This is a weak position. Exhibit the traits of a trusted advisor, and you will speed up the process of being perceived as one. Begin by expressing empathy, e.g. how difficult it must be to (fill in the blank). Use a warm, confident tone and be a good listener. Then demonstrate an understanding of your clients' business, industry or challenge. Use examples that emphasize long term associations with clients. Only after these steps have been taken can you offer advisements and have them seriously considered.

Science is nothing but developed perception, interpreted intent, common sense rounded out and minutely articulated.

George Santayana, Philosopher

TIP 61 THINK, DON'T TELL

Like a trained actor, always know what you want to achieve before speaking. Make it a simple, active statement that provides a focus and is the core of your presentation. Keep this objective primary in your thinking, but resist saying it aloud. Rather than state, "We will weather difficult times ahead and come out on top" or "Your information is not secure, but we can protect it"—think it. Be creative. Ask questions. Deliver appropriate anecdotes. Vividly illustrate the process and link it to the outcome. When your objective is your driving force, it will positively affect both language and behavior.

Obstacles are those terrible things you see when you take your eyes off the goal.

Hannah Arendt, Philosopher

TIP 62   EMOTIONAL VS COGNITIVE

In many service professions, speakers exclusively employ cognitive persuasion—utilizing analysis, reasoning and/or experience. They present robust evidence and advocate a position, often presented in a linear fashion. Content leads and personal beliefs or feelings are excised. The latest scientific research reveals we make more than 80% of our decisions emotionally and back them up intellectually. To be emotionally persuasive, connect to your audience, move yourself in front of the content, and commit to what you are passionate about.

If you would persuade, you must appeal to interest, rather than intellect.

Benjamin Franklin, Inventor, Writer, U.S. Statesman

There can be no transforming of darkness into light and of apathy into movement without emotion.

Carl Jung, Philosopher

TIP 63   WHAT'S MY MOTIVATION?

The best way to achieve your objective is to decide on your role. Am I the trusted advisor, making recommendations from a perspective of empathy and experience? Am I the motivator, encouraging my client to take action? Or is facilitator the right choice—attending to details, putting the players together and making sure the deal goes through? By choosing a specific role, you have the advantage of playing to your strength, being clear, knowing what content to deliver and what to edit out. You have differentiated yourself and are congruent with your material. An added benefit is the audience knows who you are and what's expected of them.

The whole object of comedy is to be yourself and the closer you get to that, the funnier you will be.

Jerry Seinfeld, Comedian

69

TIP 64   PROPELLER HEAD

When asked for their objective, many of our clients say it is to educate or inform. To appear professional and knowledgeable, they assume the mantle of the "expert," which denotes unassailable authority. Although expertise is inherent in every speaking role, choosing to be the expert can quickly dull a subject or overload the listener with facts and figures. Experts inform, but rarely persuade and do not encourage discourse. Especially in business, the goal is to build client relationships. To make your presentation more compelling, select a more approachable role—like trusted advisor, seasoned veteran or mobilizer.

An expert is one who knows more and more about less and less.

Nicholas Butler, U.S. Educator

Experts should be on tap, but never on top.

Winston Churchill, British Prime Minister

TIP 65   OUT FRONT

Traditional business etiquette dictates a speaker present an agenda or outline their talk in opening remarks. Eloqui disagrees. A speaker needs to stay ahead of the audience. When we know what will be covered and can predict what will be said, time seems to slow to a crawl. Imagine going to a theatre performance, the curtain rises, an actor walks on stage and says: "Glad you could join us this evening. Over the course of the next two and a half hours, you will be seeing a three act play with both comedy and drama. And oh, by the way, in the second act, the hero dies." This is not to say your presentation should be disorienting or fragmented. Rather, strive to have the audience think, "What happens next?"

I have ten commandments. The first nine are, thou shalt not bore. The tenth is, thou shalt have right of final cut.

Billy Wilder, Film Director

Speaker Survival Guide

THE TEFLON EFFECT

When you describe your firm as "full service," that you "care about your clients," or say you deal with "high net worth individuals," your phrases slide into the dustbin of mediocrity. These expressions have no real substance, sound glib, and can create distance in listeners. Challenge yourself to describe your profession, industry and services in novel ways, without general terms or shopworn phrases. The audience (or client) will appreciate your creative thinking and individuality, and you will be differentiated from the competition.

Imagination is more important than knowledge.

Albert Einstein, Scientist

As we enter a new age of business engagement, it is useful to sound as if we were having a conversation across the kitchen table, rather than lecturing from a podium. The more technical or clinical the information, the more straightforward language, comparisons and associative images will clarify content and make it come alive. The ease of informal speaking also translates into great confidence, and demonstrates you have the intelligence to make complex issues understandable and clear.

High concept involves the ability to create artistic and emotional beauty, to detect patterns and opportunities, to craft a satisfying narrative, and to come up with inventions the world didn't know it was missing.

Daniel Pink, Author, *Wired Magazine*

During a presentation, interactivity with clients is generally defined as: "We present, then ask for questions." Instead, consider the first few minutes of a tennis match, when a player serves and volleys to assess their opponent's style, strengths and weaknesses. The same evaluation and analysis is useful in business. For example, when an investment banker pitches a deal, the CEO of the company for sale may be very attached to maintaining the integrity of his corporate culture, but less interested in the valuation process. It's easy to miss important connecting points with a rigid structure or preconceived plan. Better to volley with probing questions and make assumptions to win the game.

Is sloppiness in speech caused by ignorance or apathy? I don't know, and I don't care.

William Safire, Columnist

TIP 69   ACTIVE OR PASSIVE

Your presentation can engage the listener, or create mental passivity, depending on your choice of words, syntax and objective. Lecturing, educating or informing are all passive modes which ask little from the listener. Instead, seek to inspire or persuade. Choose examples with which the audience can identify. Use language that will pique our imagination. Opt for specifics rather than generalities so we can visualize your information through the filter of our own experience. Ask questions, customize your talk, and draw in the listener.

> *If we weren't all so interested in ourselves, life would be so uninteresting we couldn't endure it.*
>
> Arthur Schopenhauer, Philosopher

© 2008 Second Edition, Eloqui

TIP 70   TEAM PRESENTING

With a partner, the first step is to delegate the presentation of content. It is especially relevant when one person traditionally takes the leadership position and does most of the talking. One person should cover big picture or strategy, while another facilitates and is responsible for process. If necessary, a third person can be the expert or analyst. Decide who leads. When PowerPoint is involved, a leader should be determined for each slide or content area. When done correctly, each person focuses on their specialty, confusion is eliminated, and the perception is that your company or team works well together.

You can have brilliant ideas, but if you can't get them across, your ideas won't get you anywhere.

Lee Iacocca, Chairman: Chrysler Corporation

Presenting as a team is an effective way to keep an audience engaged. Different perspectives, expertise and backgrounds create counterpoint. The trick is to "pass the baton" seamlessly. To effect a clean hand-off, the person speaking must definitively finish a thought, end with a downward inflection, or pause long enough for their partner to jump in. If the speaker strings phrases together, or uses run-on sentences, the other presenters are unsure of their entrance cue. With practice, there is no need to resort to more obvious signals, like head nods, hand gestures, or asking your partner to take over.

Speech is conveniently located midway between thought and action, where it often substitutes for both.

John Andrew Holmes, Author

With a partner, you can create a more dynamic presentation. Stand on the same plane, as if there were an invisible line drawn across the stage. Stand approximately one to two feet apart, depending upon the size of the room... Stay physically open to both the audience and your partner. Turn and face your partner in profile only when they will be speaking for a long time... For dramatic emphasis, walk at an angle toward the audience and in front of your partner. Rehearse this move, so your partner walks behind you, switching sides, as if you were playing doubles tennis. The goal is to return to the same plane, standing next to each other.

How difficult it is to place a figure alone on a canvas... to concentrate all the interest on this unique figure, and still keep it living and real. To paint two figures which get their interest from the duality of the two personalities is child's play in comparison.

Edouard Manet, Impressionist painter

For hand-offs to be successful, always watch your partner when they are speaking. If you make eye contact and try to assess the response of the audience, you will pull focus from the speaker. Gauging audience reaction is the speaker's responsibility... To change up the pace, when your partner stops and before you begin, leave a shorter or longer pause... If your partner finishes, and you don't know what to say, agree with or repeat the last thing said. It will give you time to collect your thoughts, or allow your partner to jump back in... Finally, while you are speaking, don't forget to periodically make eye contact with your partner, as if they were one of the audience. This will allow your partner to alert you in case they have something to say and makes their entrance smooth and natural.

I don't know anything about luck. I've never banked on it, and I'm afraid of people who do. Luck to me is something else—hard work and realizing what is opportunity and what isn't.

Lucille Ball, Comedienne and Actress

79

TIP 74   SECOND CHAIR

In a team presentation, the impact of the non-speaker cannot be overestimated. The audience's focus inevitably goes to the observer in second chair, as we look for signals to determine their response to and connection with the speaker. Since much will be decided by non-verbal cues, it is imperative for the non-speaker to face, stay open to, and focus on first chair. To encourage assent, occasionally nod and smile. While listening, consider what the audience wants to know, and be ready to ask the question, or comment on the issue, when it is your turn. This interplay will engineer the perception that you respect and appreciate one another.

A good listener is not only popular everywhere, but after a while, he gets to know something.

Wilson Mizner, Screenwriter

A good listener is usually thinking about something else.

Kin Hubbard, Author

TIP 75   HEAR HERE

The number one client complaint is not being heard. If you fail to interview a client on their needs, or do not address their challenges, you're speaking for your own benefit, not theirs. Being a good listener is essential to closing a business deal. Techniques for successful cueing and listening include probing for specifics; incorporating answers immediately into the conversation; and periodically recapping (without saying "to recap") key points to assess their viability. Demonstrate your preparedness by floating assumptions, even if they're wrong. When the client corrects you, they are engaged and as long as you don't get defensive, you can engineer a successful dialogue.

Only in quiet waters do things mirror themselves undistorted. Only in a quiet mind is adequate perception of the world.
Hans Margolius, Former UN Chief Weapons Inspector in Iraq

Speaker Survival Guide

TIP 76   LEADERSHIP

You can be exceptionally talented in your chosen field, but if you do not speak publicly on your topic, or motivate your team through speech—career advancement is limited. We look to leaders to guide and inspire us with their words and actions. To demonstrate command presence, be aware of your posture. Lift your chin slightly and imagine a string pulling your chest out one inch. Speak in measured tones. Short punchy phrases are better than long ones. Make eye contact around the room. Exhibit congruency in language and behavior. And express the courage of your convictions.

Our words have wings but fly not where we would.

George Eliot, Author and Poet

TIP 77   JARGON

Specific industries or businesses may be accustomed to using slang or jargon as language shortcuts. And while the speaker understands the meaning and broader implication of these terms, their use can create distance, confusion and resentment for anyone outside the inner circle. Strive to describe your services and messages with expressive language. Don't take the easy way and fall back on overused, trite expressions or insider terminology. Use colorful analogies, especially those that paint a sharp picture or clarify the relationship of your ideas.

> *The intuitive appeal of a scientific theory has to do with how well its metaphors fit one's experience.*
>
> George Lakoff, Linguist and
> Author of *Don't Think of an Elephant*

Speaker Survival Guide

Speakers assume by being general, they are inclusive and polite. Unfortunately, delivering a menu of services gives everything equal weight and diminishes the impact. Example: "We are a full service firm, specializing in wealth management for high net worth individuals." This statement does not distinguish the speaker, nor does it convey what their firm actually does. One useful gauge is whether or not your competitor can say the same thing. Better to focus on one aspect of your business, and allow the listener to build a picture over time of you and your services. Details are triggers to create this visual snapshot and crisply differentiate the speaker.

An abstract idea goes in one ear and out the other— never establishing itself unless reinforced by a picture or story.

Winston Churchill, British Prime Minister

TIP 79   VARIATIONS ON A THEME

The dictionary defines "theme" as an idea, point of view or perception embodied and expanded upon in a work of art. In classical music, a theme is the principal melody, although each time you hear it, the instrumentation and tempo is different. When speaking, a theme is an easily repeatable phrase, which denotes the central idea of your presentation, e.g. "gifts come in unexpected packages" or "intellectual property is the real estate of the 21st century." Each time you revisit your theme, illuminate a new aspect of the content. Memorable themes serve to ground abstract concepts and simplify complex ideas.

Experience is a jewel, and it had need be so, for it is often purchased at an infinite rate.

William Shakespeare, Playwright

I'm afraid of storms, for I'm learning to sail my ship.

Louisa May Alcott, Author of *Little Women*

© 2008 Second Edition, Eloqui

PowerPoint is best used to tell a story, but has become a crutch or cueing device. Typically, slides are so text rich, by the time the audience reads them, the speaker has finished their commentary. Since you cannot compete with the big screen, keep the content spare, use fewer slides, and never read what's on the screen. Instead, interpret the data, giving a key message or take-a-way. When it first appears, let the audience read the slide for about 2 seconds. To regain focus, make a strong move or gesture, or raise your voice... Build the data, rather than having it appear all at once... Keep the titles short... Highlight or use a contrasting color for key phrases... Occasionally go to a blank screen to regain the focus and change the pacing. And whenever possible, use visual images to support your narrative.

Too many slides make audiences sleepy.

Richard Nixon, U.S. President

We've observed a tendency in business presentations to use generic phrases, like "we help our clients" or "we're creative problem solvers" which have no real meaning. Be specific about your services to reinforce your unique qualities. Another over-used phrase is "I'm going to talk about," when the speaker is already talking. Why say "Over the next 20 minutes, I will cover…" when, like Nike, you can "just do it!" Resist the temptation to pick up phrases and idioms from your colleagues. Effective speakers personalize their comments and are unique in their descriptive powers.

We think in generalities, but we live in detail.
Alfred North Whitehead, Mathematician and Philosopher

Speakers sometimes detract from their presentations by using verbal shorthand or general phrases. These phrases may once have had meaning or cachet, but are now outdated and overused. Examples: "In terms of... Basically... At the end of the day... I was going to... State of the art... World class... High tech... or 24/7." If you hear yourself use general phrases, follow them up with a "like", "such as" or "for example". Or better yet, consider a more compelling and unique way to express your thought or idea.

The right to express ideas, good ideas, bad ideas, wild ideas, crazy ideas, impossible ideas—this is the most precious right the individual can have.

Dalton Trumbo, Screenwriter

TIP 83 LITMUS TEST

How do you assess if you've met your speaking objective? One barometer is the questions you do or don't receive. For example, if you're asked for projections or technical data, the audience perceives you as an expert... If you're asked how you accomplished a project, you're perceived as a veteran... Similarly, wanting to know what resources you would utilize is a question for a mobilizer... And a trusted advisor is the appropriate source for recommendations or advisements. After your next talk, make a mental note of the questions and decide which role will best accomplish your goal in the future.

I have learned throughout my life as a composer chiefly through my mistakes and pursuits of false assumptions, not by my exposure to founts of wisdom and knowledge.

Igor Stravinsky, Composer

Media Savvy

Sound Bites
The Medium
Reach through the Lens

TIP 84   SOUND BITES

Before going on camera, distill your
message into three key points. Practice
delivering these points without prefatory
wind-ups or fillers. Whatever question the
interviewer asks, be ready to redirect and
segue to those key points. Don't waste time
with unnecessary explanations, too many
details or context. Television interviews
thrive on 20 second sound bites. The
interviewer can always do a follow-up, so
make your statements succinct, colorful
and definitive. This is your opportunity to
make an impact and tease the viewer so
they will want more.

My main goal is to tell a story.

Stephen Sondheim, Composer

Talk low. Talk slow. And don't say too much.

John Wayne, Actor

The television studio is a world unto itself.
Focus only on your interview and avoid the
distractions of lights, crew and monitors.
Whenever possible, walk the space and sit
in the chair before air time. Bring your
own MAC Studio make-up kit and be
proficient in applying it. This goes for men
as well as women. Be familiar with the
interview questions. Warm up by speaking
to your host, or rehearsing your answers in
front of the camera or monitor. Drink
room temperature water. Breathe. And
remind yourself of the positive impact you
will have on the viewers.

*Keep things informal. Talking is the natural way to
do business. Writing is great for keeping records and
putting down details, but talk generates ideas.*

T. Boone Pickens, Businessman

TIP 86 REACH THROUGH THE LENS

When appearing on camera, be aware of more than your words. The camera picks up subtle cues in your expression, tone and posture. Wear simple colors and patterns so the attention goes to your face. Make a positive mental connection with the individual asking the questions. If you are speaking directly into the camera, project the identity of a person onto the lens and use a conversational tone. When asked a question, maintain eye contact with the interviewer, nod and look thoughtful. Take a beat before answering. And with tough questions, use self effacing humor and charm.

Anything I've ever done that ultimately was worthwhile… initially scared me to death.

Betty Bender, Teacher

93

Find Your Authentic Voice

Through Line
Engineer Perception
Common Thread
Snowflake
Typecast
Generalization
Persuasive Blend
Accent the Positive

Critical Acumen
Likeability Quotient
Diamond in the Rough
Eloquence
Strong Suit
Non-Verbal Cues
Congruity

TIP 87   THROUGH LINE

An actor prepares for a role by creating the
back story or the character's history. What
they look for are behavioral motifs that
shape the personality, gestures and voice.
When a speaker infuses their talk with
values and personal anecdotes, they are
communicating their own through line—the
elements that have shaped and formed their
character. And like a well researched acting
performance, this authenticity gives the
speaker gravitas and a high believability
quotient.

The longest journey
Is the journey inwards
Of him who has chosen his destiny.

Dag Hammarskjold, Statesman

Speaker Survival Guide

TIP 88   ENGINEER PERCEPTION

From the moment you enter a room or walk to the stage, people pick up signals about you and your competence. No matter how uncomfortable you feel, make a conscious decision to exhibit easy confidence and enjoyment of speaking. An exercise called "sense memory" is instrumental in achieving this goal. Select a particular incident from your past when you exhibited the specific quality you would like to convey, e.g. relaxed, authoritative, or excited. Recall the incident in vivid detail, using all of your senses. When you retrieve that experience just prior to speaking, you demonstrate the specific trait you want the audience to perceive.

Perception is strong and sight weak. In strategy it is important to see distant things as if they were close and to take a distanced view of close things.

Miyamoto Musashi, Japanese Samurai

© 2008 Second Edition, Eloqui

TIP 89   COMMON THREAD

Although very different in temperament, style and approach, great speakers throughout history draw from a common gene pool of techniques. As master storytellers, they utilize anecdotes with vivid details; quote eloquent thinkers; incorporate themes which are revisited with variation; deliver compelling opens and closes; and project their unique personalities, regardless of the style of the day. For example, the author Calvin Trillin rhymes his messages and peppers his talk with um's. Memorable speakers exhibit three universal traits— certainty (the courage of their convictions), being present, and playing to their strengths.

For the ordinary to become extraordinary it must be seen differently, afresh.

Daniel Farber, Photographer

There is no "one size fits all" public speaking or communication model. Human behavior is complex, and individuals are unique. Like a novelist, seek to identify and develop your own distinctive voice. To be effective, everything you observe must be translated into your own style, rather than copied or imitated. Napoleon never tried to cover up his thick Corsican accent, and Churchill was unapologetically irascible and stuttered. We attract business, friends and associates when we understand what defines us and are clear and confident in our expression.

This above all, to thine own self be true;
And it must follow, as the night the day,
Thou canst not then be false to any man…

Polonius in Hamlet
William Shakespeare, Playwright

TIP 91 TYPE CAST

We hear and speak through one of four communication filters.

Artisan: "Bottom-line me"… or "Just the facts ma'am"

Guardian: "Cite precedent and tell me how it's organized"

Rational: "Lead with context, or I won't follow you"

Idealist: "Identify the contribution and connection to the greater meaning"

Address these filters, and you will not have to wonder if you have reached your audience. We use language consistent with our type, so the Guardian links or compares subjects; the Artisan gives colorful, brief anecdotes; the Idealist is metaphoric, speaking in global terms; and the Rational gives a detailed description, providing both the setting and how elements interact.

> *The actor should never listen to the words but listen to the person.*
>
> Jack Lemmon, Actor

© 2008 Second Edition, Eloqui

GENERALIZATION

When a speaker is visibly awkward or uncomfortable, we assume they will exhibit the same discomfort or insecurity when conducting business. In psychology, this is called generalization training. While this may be an unfair assumption, you can use it to your advantage. Before your presentation, remind yourself to appear confident and in charge. Speak with conviction. Control your physical space. Your goal is to make your audience believe you conduct business with the same authority. Until it's second nature: fake it till you make it.

All that a man does outwardly is but the expression and completion of his inward thought. To work effectually, he must think clearly; to act nobly, he must think nobly…

William E. Channing, Unitarian Minister

TIP 93   PERSUASIVE BLEND

People make the mistake of believing that to be persuasive, they simply need to present strong evidence. The truth is you can't beat people up with intellect. Pure, rational argument, however robust, is limited. As a speaker, you want your audience to trust and believe you, then identify with your topic, and when appropriate, take action. It takes a blend of emotional and cognitive persuasion to achieve this level of buy-in.

The mind makes a decision based on agreement with the information the speaker provides. The heart makes the commitment based on a feeling of connection to the leader. The mind looks for evidence, the heart looks for passion.

Terry Pearce, Author of *Leading out Loud*

Speaker Survival Guide

TIP 94   ACCENT THE POSITIVE

We all reveal our place of birth through speech, specifically the shape of our vowels and the rhythm of our syntax. Although broadcasters are trained to eliminate all trace of regional dialect, being accent free is not necessarily an advantage. The ear is attracted by the anomaly or musicality of our different voices. However, to make yourself perfectly understood, study voice and diction, slow down and enunciate clearly. Rather than being passive, the audience imagines our background and cultural heritage. When we are comfortable with ourselves, this is a positive.

While one should always study the method of a great artist, one should never imitate his manner. The manner of an artist is essentially individual, the method of an artist is absolutely universal. The first is personality, which no one should copy; the second is perfection, which all should aim at.

Oscar Wilde, Playwright

Watch and listen to your favorite news anchors, politicians, comedians and performers. Do they sound authentic? Can they tell a good story? Take note of their physical presence, phrasing, and listening skills which appeal to you. Jeff Prather, an author on Northwest wines and wine educator in Napa Valley has a recipe for developing your palate. "Pay attention to what you like, take notes and look for patterns that reflect your taste." When you apply the same technique to speaking, you broaden your range and like an aged wine, exhibit complexity and harmony.

> *I'm a dramatist of songs. I have to observe and try to understand the space in which the songs exist, the root. They're more than words and notes. To me, they are a whole lot of little, tiny vignettes of people and places and characters going through a particular thing.*
>
> Roger Daltry, Lead Singer of The Who

TIP 96   LIKEABILITY QUOTIENT

A study on Impression Management and Interpersonal Behavior assessed a speaker's "likeability quotient." The two most important factors for being likeable and memorable were: In their opening remarks, a speaker revealed something about themselves or their perspective, and the presentation was always tailored to the specific audience. We are hard wired to accept ideas from and do business with people we like and trust. To enhance your success, remember the likeability quotient when constructing your next presentation.

> *CEOs are reluctant to tell stories about themselves. But when you share a bit of yourself with others, you win their trust and affection, and they will more readily buy into what you are promoting.*
>
> James C. Humes, Speechwriter for 3 Presidents

DIAMOND IN THE ROUGH

There is a widely held belief that being polished and having a prepared text is a prerequisite for successful speaking. To that end, presenters will write, rehearse, and even memorize their material. Although the resulting delivery is smooth, the spontaneity and excitement has been drained from the talk. Instead, identify your intention—then deliver it in your own words. Craft your opening and close. But be in the moment, so that you're able to sense the audience's reaction. Be brave and incorporate a fresh observation or response to what you're sensing. When you truly connect with your audience, they feel as if the presentation is extemporaneous and has been prepared specifically for them.

Words calculated to catch everyone, may catch no one.
Adlai Stevenson Jr., Democrat and U.S. diplomat

© 2008 Second Edition, Eloqui   ***Speaker Survival Guide***

Eloquent speech is often mistaken for rococo, florid prose. When you try to express an idea with too many words, you lose the thread or flow under the weight of verbal mass. If your motivation is to move people, to give your ideas substance, consider your closely held beliefs. Eloquence is about the underlying convictions, which are your passion. And conviction is best delivered with economy. A clear idea, simply stated, is elegant and potent.

No man has the right to dictate what other men should perceive, create or produce, but all should be encouraged to reveal themselves, their perceptions and emotions, and to build confidence in the creative spirit.

Ansel Adams, Photographer

TIP 99 STRONG SUIT

The traditional business paradigm says never inject personal views into a presentation. Revealing your take on a subject, or how you have been affected personally makes a speaker vulnerable. But vulnerability has great rewards. It quickly establishes your trustworthiness and authenticity. As a speaker, it requires introspection. And it takes courage—fighting the fear you will be exposed, ridiculed or not taken seriously. Yet, once you have established authenticity, you can influence people toward change, contracting your services, or accepting your point of view.

When we were children, we used to think that when we were grown-up we would no longer be vulnerable. But to grow up is to accept vulnerability... To be alive is to be vulnerable.

Madeleine L'Engle, Author of *A Wrinkle in Time*

What we don't say speaks volumes. Do you point with a closed fist or single finger to emphasize a point? Do you fidget with your fingernails, roll your shoulders, or sit back and cross your arms and legs when listening to someone? When you move in a space, do you wander aimlessly or rock back and forth? An audience reads body language and physical gestures to assess who we are, what we want and what they think of us. Videotape or look in a mirror for what you are telegraphing. Feature your authenticity and unique qualities, not your tics and mannerisms. The goal is to create a complementary marriage of words and gestures.

> *Five senses; an incurably abstract intellect; a haphazardly selective memory; a set of preconceptions and assumptions so numerous that I can never examine more than a minority of them — never become conscious of them all. How much of total reality can such an apparatus let through?*
>
> C. S. Lewis, Author of *Narnian Chronicles*

TIP 101 CONGRUITY

When our personal and business lives are not in alignment, few of us are talented enough to hide it. When speaking, you will most likely suffer from stage fright—the fear of being found out or discovered as a fake and the audience will sense your discomfort. Imbue your presentations with personal values, ideas and true emotion. Although not everyone will agree with you or always respond favorably, you will embody integrity and authenticity. The personal pay-off and immeasurable gift is that you are true to yourself.

People will forget what you said, people will forget what you did, but people will never forget how you made them feel.

Maya Angelou, Author and Poet

Speaker Survival Guide